FROM THE INSIDE OUT

An Awakening

Royce,

Choices:
Minimum Achievements
or
Maximum Potential

Michael Krafthond

FROM THE INSIDE OUT

An Awakening

Michael Everhart

?Y

QUESTION Y PUBLISHING

HOUSTON, TEXAS 77244

FROM THE INSIDE OUT: An Awakening
Copyright © 2003 by Michael Everhart. All rights reserved.
No part of this book may be reproduced, stored in retrieval
systems or transmitted in any form, by any means, including
mechanical, electronic, photocopying, recording or otherwise,
without prior written permission of the publisher.

QUESTION Y PUBLISHING books may be purchased at a
special discount when ordered in bulk quantities. For more
information please write QUESTION Y PUBLISHING P.O. Box
442005, Houston, TX 77244-2005 or visit our website at
www.QUESTIONY.com
For immediate response email qypublishing@sbcglobal.net

FROM THE INSIDE OUT

Cover Designed by Avery Matthews

Book Layout by La Tonya Holman

Poetic Layout by Robin Porter

Edited by Roger Leslie

ISBN: 0-9740126-0-2

PRINTED IN THE UNITED STATES OF AMERICA.

Acknowledgements

I would like to thank GOD for bestowing blessings upon me, for without the guidance of my Lord, my inner voice, I would be nothing. I have been blessed with the support and help from so many people that it would be impossible to list them all. However, I must give special thanks to a few people for taking the time to help make this project a success:

Book Layout:
La Tonya Holman, for her bold initiative and unwavering dedication. She played an instrumental role in every aspect of this project from start to finish.

Cover Design:
Avery Matthews, for his patience through the many revisions of the book cover.

Creative Inspiration:
Chandrika Jones, Douglas Perry, and Robin C. Porter, for their inspiration. They have taught me that the pen is truly mightier than the sword.

Critics Preview and Afterthoughts:
Terri J. Anderson, Latoya Y. Guidry, Yolanda Herring, Na'Teasel La'Taye Hinton, La Tonya Holman, Becky Tyner Hood, LaKenya Perry, Dr. Ronald J. Peters, and TeKedra A. Pierre, for their unbiased comments. Their suggestions have been instrumental in helping me to more clearly express my thoughts.

Editing:
Roger Leslie, for his expertise and global feedback.

Environment:
Family, Friends, Classmates, Teammates, Coaches, Mentors and Coworkers, for their love and support.

Poetic Layout:
Robin Porter, for her creative advice and suggestions.

Think Tank:
Shajuana Berry, Ambrose Brooks, Tiffany Carter, Na'Teasel La'Taye Hinton, La Tonya Holman, Larry O'Neal, and LaKenya Perry, for their many different viewpoints on life.

Web Design:
Jamal Williams, for his creative vision, technical support, and flexibility on such a short notice.

MESSAGE TO THE READER

I have done a review for the author; this review is for the reader. This review to you the reader is based on content and my personal interpretation. I do not know the author personally, however his work is very personal.

FROM THE INSIDE OUT *is a book I became interested in after reading a small portion. I read a few passages and thought, "I have to read this". Shortly thereafter I expressed my interest to the author and received the book in its' entirety. It did not take long to read through the first time. I made an instant and memorable connection with the author and his work. The book flows like warm water out of a faucet; uninterrupted. I eagerly turned page after page looking for more.*

This book is a good personal developmental reading that includes parables and spoken word in order to stimulate the mind. The anticipated and climactic conclusion in selections like "Incomplete" causes one to jump up and take control of his/her own life. Parables such as "Butterfly" and "Lion" allow us to look deeper within ourselves and find our true purpose and meaning.

Upon completion of this book, I made new realizations about many things including life itself. Each phase allowed me to see more than I had before. I know this will pull many thoughts and emotions out of you as it did for me. As the author states "An inside out approach will not only cause us to question why we should do things, but also help us to discover our true passion". Thank you, I found one.

Teke

CONTENTS

"INCOMPLETE"………………………………...........1
INTRODUCTION……………………………….....5
PHASE 1-
NO EVOLUTION WITHOUT A REVOLUTION……...13
    "QUE"…………………………………………*22*

PHASE 2-
REWARDS WITHOUT RISK……………………....**25**
    "JACK"………………………………………...*32*

PHASE 3-
NO DEDICATION WITHOUT DETERMINATION…..**37**
    "SOLUTIONS"……………………………....*48*
    "EAGLE"………………………………....…*54*

PHASE 4-
PURPOSE……………………………………....*59*
    "BUTTERFLY"……………………………....*70*

PHASE 5-
COMPETING TO COLLABORATING……………....**75**
    "TREES"……………………………………*85*

PHASE 6-
WALKING THE TALK……………………………**89**
    "LION"……………………………………*95*

PHASE 7-
DREAM AND REFLECT………………………...**99**
    "LOVE"…………………………………*104*
    "APOLOGY"……………………………*108*
    "RANDOM THOUGHTS" ………………*111*

MESSAGE FROM THE AUTHOR……………....…..*116*

INCOMPLETE ?

I wish I could meet the man,
That came up with the saying,
"Always have a backup plan".

Maybe it's not his fault,
Maybe it's just that I was taught,
Something very contrary
to what he originally thought.

But, what about this though,
I know you heard this before,
"Always diversify your portfolio"

Right now I'm filled with resentment,
Keep finding myself in this same predicament,
Unable to put forth my all,
Issues unresolved,
I'm incapable of forming a commitment.

How can I ever become one with myself,
when I am constantly in a state of division,
My judgment is altered
Which falters my precision,
Ultimately affecting my decisions.

I tell myself I'm giving a 100 percent,
But as long as the percent is split,
I can be good in this
And possibly, even that,
but greatness will never exist,

Looking back over the days,
I realize that I've become,
This jack of all trades,
Yet a master of none.

Introduction

When it's all said and done,
I realize that, I have to let go,
Stop creating back doors,
Or escape routes,
Because I'm filled with doubt,
Afraid to be without,
Only one thing left to do, shout out!

STOP!!!!!

This is easier said than done,
But the process has already begun,
Sometimes I feel as if I've gotten no where,
Until I compare where I'm at to where I'm from,

But the answers to this will complete me,
Or else the fear of failure will defeat me,
At night when I fall to my knees to pray,
I'm asking, "Please Lord, will you teach me",

'Cause I understand the ratio of risk to success,
But I feel like a fish out of water, without my safety net,
My walls close in, I'm filled with stress,
The last thing I want to hear is "He still lost,
After giving his best",

Everything in life, is a lesson or a blessing,
So no need to keep questioning,

Just relax, allow your mind to start digesting,
And embracing the laws of nature, or the karma,
That's keep knocking at your armor,
Trying to get in
Up under your skin
But you're afraid because you view this as a form of

Weakness,

And your fear is what keeps you,
In a cage
Filled with rage
No different than a slave,
Unable to put this fear beneath you,

I'm incomplete it seems,
No plan, no scheme,
No peace on earth
No peace in my dreams,
I feel like a fiend,
Thinking of one thing,
Holler out and scream!

STOP!!!!!!!!

I'm Incomplete?

Introduction

INTRODUCTION

How it All Begins

Do you remember having a dream or talent? Have you allowed lack of money, fear of failure, lack of support, lack of time, or fear of change to handicap you? First, you go to work to maintain your current level of comfort. Next, you go home and spend a couple of hours with your family. Finally, you rush to bed to get some sleep so that you can awake to repeat the same cycle. Do you look forward to the weekends because you try to enjoy a week's worth of life in the two days allotted to you?

Maybe you already realize it's time to make a change but how? You can't imagine living another five years talking to your friends about the same problems that seem to have no solution. You long to spend your life doing something that you enjoy, which will continue to give you a comfortable living. You've just come to realize that you can never be happy without a sense of purpose and have grown anxious to find yours.

One day I awoke and found myself staring in the mirror trying to figure out who I was looking at.

Judging by societal standards I was doing great. Based on my background, I had defied all the laws of nature. I had successfully become not only the first person in my family to obtain a college degree, but I had also taken it a step farther and received my Masters in Business Administration before my 26th birthday.

From the *outside looking in*, it appeared as if I had it all. The truth was I had no idea what to do or where I was headed. I completed all the tasks that everyone said I should to become successful, but nothing seemed to go my way. It just didn't add up to me. I could never figure out why I spent five years in school getting a bachelor's degree to make $18,000 per year. I compared my situation to some of my friends who had entered the work force right out of high school who in five years were making more. Maybe I needed more how-to lessons.

After a year of contemplating on what I should do, I finally decided to go back to school to get my MBA. It took an additional two years to complete the coursework and obtain the degree. I quickly found out that although I had education, I lacked experience. I ended up with a job earning $30,000 a year. Within the same three years, those friends who had never thought of college were making an hourly rate equal to my salary. All those years of school taught me one thing well, how to rationalize.

I surrounded myself with the type of people that I grew up with but had mentally outgrown. In this way, I could establish a false sense of confidence by telling myself that I was successful when compared to them. In reality, I didn't make any more money than my friends, but I rationalized it by continuing to tell myself that the emphasis was not on how much money I made, but on how I made my money. Actually, I was right, but for the wrong reasons.

I falsely led myself to believe that I had a wealth of knowledge that my friends and family didn't have. Even if I was right, I didn't apply any of the knowledge. The only difference between them and me was that I continued to hold on to this passion of being successful. My unrealized dreams caused me to carry around this guilty conscious of being an under-achiever. From the *outside looking in*, that morning I realized that I was living a lie.

Over the next two years I was lost in a search of how to find something for nothing. I read several get rich quick books. They all promised a great amount of wealth with minimal time and effort. I've found this promise to be grossly incorrect. They falsely define wealth as the harvest reaped. I've learned over time that true wealth has more to do with the seeds that are planted.

From the *outside looking in*, anyone can tell you <u>what</u> to do to become successful. This type of information is directive. It can be compared to the effectiveness of good managers. Good managers tell their people what to do and how to do it. A manager's primary job is to ensure consistency in the day to day operations of the business. It took me forever to figure out that I didn't need a manager to tell me <u>what</u> to do; I needed a leader to teach me how to look within myself to find out <u>why</u> I needed to do these things.

Consistency does not exist in the real world. Effective leaders know that they cannot always be there to make decisions when change arises. Thus, they have to equip their team to think for themselves. We become equipped to adjust to the obstacles of change once we establish the <u>why</u> for doing something.

For instance, I can tell you point blank, that if you plan to truly read this book and attempt to embrace a portion of the suggestions, you may as well stop right now and estimate a budget for your new wardrobe. In preparation for your success, I just told you <u>what</u> you should do. Most of you reading this are looking for change. You have taken proactive steps to break the cycle of complacency by seeking information. You are eager to find your path, so I am sure some of you would be willing to take my advice and try something new.

A portion of you would take the initiative to go out and pick up a couple of outfits. I am equally sure that some of you have unknowingly coupled my directions with something familiar from your past. For example, you may have heard the saying, "dress for success". It is normal human tendency for us to attempt to link new and old information. If that has been the case then some of you have made the assumption that dressing for success is my reasoning for asking you to buy new clothes.

Introduction

Now allow me to explain _why_ I want you to estimate a budget for a new wardrobe. The goal of this book is to influence you to take an _inside out_ approach in evaluating your goals, defining success, and discovering your purpose in life. My gamble is that if you are successful at a few of the phases listed in the book, you will be so consumed in the newfound sense of urgency that you will lose ten pounds in the process. Thus, you will need a new wardrobe because you have under-grown your old wardrobe.

By simply telling you _what_ to do, I would have misled you to buy more clothes that were not going to be useful. The _why_ gives you a better understanding of when and under what circumstances you need to purchase the clothes. Only telling the _what_ is a sales tactic that keeps us blind about the future. It keeps us coming back for more direction and makes us hesitant to take initiative. Explaining the _whys_ gives us the ability to reason the probable future outcomes. This is the key that will free us from the cycle of treading water, in hopes that someone will save us. An explanation of _why_ is the first step in turning dreams to reality; it forces us to swim towards the shore taking destiny into our own hands.

Most of the books and seminars on <u>how</u> to become rich and successful would have been good guides if change didn't occur. If everything remained consistent as it was during the time of the so-called experts' experiences, we could conceivably follow their guidelines to our destination. It just so happens that change is one of the few things guaranteed in life. An *inside out* approach will not only cause us to question <u>why</u> we should do things, but also help us discover our true passion. This newfound sense of purpose will leave us motivated and fulfilled by the new choices we'll make.

As we revisit my journey through the seven phases, *from the inside out,* you will begin to discover your strengths and purpose in life. Your dreams will awaken as your passion for living is renewed. You will know that the time to act is now. The feeling of "Incomplete" will soon become a memory.

Introduction

PHASE ONE

"Realization" There is No Evolution Without a Revolution!

"Desire is the key to motivation, but it's determination and commitment to an unrelenting pursuit of your goal – a commitment to excellence – that will enable you to attain the success you seek."

--- *Mario Andretti*

This phase explores how to tap into your dreams to find your true passion detailing the role of goals in the process.

In the first phase of evolution *from the inside out,* the most important lesson was learning to overcome all my mental barriers and crutches. I could see myself growing away from and transcending my old ways of thinking. Facing and conquering my past limitations, showed me that life was simply what one makes of it.

Realization

Realization starts when we grow tired of the norms and begin to ponder possibilities. We begin to seek to redefine the simple definitions of life.

Questions such as "What is happiness?" and "What is success?" begin to move to the forefront of our thinking. Once we defined happiness by the way other people and things made us feel. We now start to embrace the idea that happiness is simply the ability to find a positive in any given situation. It becomes evident that we can no longer allow our race, environment, lack of love, or lack of support to limit our realistic dreams.

Most of us have a closet full of dreams separated into realizable and unrealizable. Unrealizable dreams are normally in the back of our subconscious closets hidden away and often forgotten. Most of our peers view these passions as unrealistic, making it hard for them to provide us with the mental support that we need. Unrealizable dreams are obtainable but they require dedication, patience, and commitment. Regardless, we secretly remain passionate about these dreams. We will never feel complete until we make strides towards realizing them.

Realizable dreams are usually the dreams that society dictates would be a good fit for us based on the labels that we inherit because of our race, environment, religion, etc. When we think of our realizable dreams, we often misinterpret the word "realizable" to mean something that we realize. However, in this sense, "realizable" emphasizes the dream is obtainable with moderate effort. For me, these dreams were reinforced every time I would hear someone say, "You would make a great teacher or coach." Often when we settle for pursuing realizable dreams, we seldom give 100 percent effort. Instead, we do just enough to get by or to be considered good at our job. We are not performing at our optimal level.

A passive approach would be to accept those things that society defines as realizable dreams and try to make the best of our predefined box. An aggressive approach involves going to the opposite end of the spectrum and rebelling against the norm. This approach would challenge us to dig out all the dreams locked away in the back of our closets and go after them all. In this approach the result would be similar to that of a hungry man chasing after two chickens. He will continue to starve because he is incapable of committing himself to capturing one chicken.

Phase 1: Realization

For now, it is important to know that we must choose to take neither a passive nor an aggressive approach. We must first evaluate our talents honestly. A realistic observation of ourselves helps us find a correlation between our true talents and our true dreams. Next, we must take an assertive approach to using our talents to achieve success. Many of us have a wide range of hobbies and interest and most of us have become pretty good in our optional activities. We are quick to move from one project to the next showing our competence in each subject. The ending result is that we know a little bit about much and a great deal about very little.

Choosing the talent that will best bring about our success is like choosing a meal. We can go to the buffet and sample every dish on the menu but we would be foolish to expect the same quality of food that comes from a specialty restaurant. There's nothing wrong with being a jack of all trades but we must understand that success is more closely related to that which requires the discipline to see something through, start to finish. Mastery of any subject starts with learning to set goals.

Why Set Goals?

The evolution starts when we begin to formulate goals. I'm sure everyone's heard of the importance of setting goals, but let's briefly examine the reason why it's important. Setting goals has a way of building our confidence. True self-confidence develops as we prove our abilities to ourselves. Once we are convinced, the energy radiates outward to the world like ripples in a pond. Every small success builds confidence. Therefore, it is important for us to sit down and write out a plan. Goals can start in the form of a schedule. The schedule creates the habit of accomplishing small goals on a daily basis while strengthening our self-discipline. We are what we repeatedly do. The most truthful email that I ever read stated:

> *"Our thoughts transform into our words, and our words become our actions, which transform into habits. The habits that we build today represent our character of tomorrow, which is manifested in our destiny."*
>
> *---Anonymous*

Goals become realistic when we base them on our true talents and skills. By adding time

Phase 1: Realization

constraints, we give ourselves a target or deadline that serves to weaken procrastination. How many times have we said that we were going to do something, but never established a deadline? Most times, we know exactly <u>what</u> we need to do, but have failed to put thoughts into action. We are hesitant because we have yet to convince ourselves <u>why</u> we should do it. I call this purgatory. We have not failed, but we have yet to succeed. We are ultimately lost in a world of excuses. We have to learn to build our confidence with short successes that allow us to take on bigger and more risky tasks. It inspires the belief that if things do go wrong, we can make them right by using our abilities.

We should start with some of the simplest goals and then question why we want these particular items until we arrive at that which we truly desire. The first thought that comes to most of our minds is that money would be the answer to all our woes. "If we could just make enough money to get this or payoff that, then we could concentrate on this." If we would just take the time to question why we need money, we could come up with a better idea of what we really need.

There are several reasons why we need more money, but one of the most common reasons is so that we can have a better opportunity to enjoy life. If this is the case, money is not the focal point; it is merely a means to an end. Obtaining money is simply a step of a process that was predefined by someone other than us; thus we should not make it our focal point. A better opportunity to enjoy life means different things to different people, but for some it means freeing up time and finding our true passion. Time away from work allows us to pursue our passion giving birth to creativity in the process.

Why We Must Maximize Our Time

For a moment, let's take a brief journey back in time to the era of the hunter-gatherer. During this period, the tribe's primary focus was trying to accumulate food for survival. I compare this with going to work for eight to ten hours a day. By accident, humans learned to become farmers. This discovery freed them from the chore of roaming the countryside in search of their next meal. They discovered that by concentrating their efforts they could generate enough food to last them throughout the winter. They were free to turn their interests to other pursuits. Many historians suggest that this free time gave birth to art, writing and religion.

If the saying is true, "the rich get richer and the poor get poorer," it's because the rich spend their time coming up with creative ideas to make more money while the poor continue to work for survival. It's amazing what a few moments of reflection can do for us. We don't have to wait for an accidental discovery like the farmers; we can create our opportunities by taking the necessary risk to free up time.

Why Embrace the Revolution?

We should come to the conclusion that we have to first find our true passion and desire. Few have found something worth fighting for, but once we find it, the rewards become worth the risk. Secondly, we must act. We've been drenched with the idea that knowledge is power; however, we manifest our power only when we act upon our knowledge. I'm sure many of us have read the email that was mentioned earlier, but most of us have remained dormant in the

Phase 1: Realization

transition of thought to words, refusing to go any farther.

In this phase, the most important thing that I learned was that we can't afford to sit by and wait for things to change or wait for people to grant us opportunities. We can't just do the necessary things prescribed by society as the steps for success and think that it will happen for us. All evolution or change is the result of a revolution. Every generation needs a new revolution inspired by passion. One man/woman filled with passion is a far greater asset than forty with lukewarm enthusiasm. We should never doubt that it takes but a small group to change the world, take a lesson from Que.

Phase 1: Realization

QUE

There once was a courageous dog,
his friends called him Que,
He existed in a time long before humans,
even dinosaurs, too.

Que was a special dog with goals that stemmed from a body of dreams,
His passion
His fire,
His ultimate desire,
was to become a member of the "Mighty Dog Team".

The story takes place in the form of a rhyme,
Done by design,
In order to tap into your mind,
And take you back in time

To a place,
where there was no purpose for the brain,
Because the canine/the dog,
was at the top of the food chain.

In this day and time,
the gauge for success,
Was measured by the roar of the bark that wailed from the dog's chest,

In essence this meant success was something that was out of one's control,
One was either born with it, or without it,
at least that's how it was told.

But Que was a different dog,
he refused to believe,
He took advice from a wise teacher who said,
"An open mind is the key."

Phase 1: Realization

Along his path in the search for truth,
he bumped into an old friend named Chris.
"The only place that you find success before work is in the dictionary"
Chris told him this.

Meanwhile, the Mighty Dog Team,
which was considered the elite,
Had this roaring growl in their barks
that made a sound so sweet.

This was the day for new dogs,
to bark their way into the group.
The initiation process was almost over.
Then came Que.

He had a fire in his eyes,
for he had found the key.
He learned from that inner voice that said,
"When you decide to make a stand, die empty!"

As he approached the stage in his heart he knew,
Although success wasn't born within him,
it was something that grew.

As he stepped upon the stage,
in a rage he rebelled,
"There is no evolution without a revolution!"
To the crowd, he yelled.

In the hearts of all the common dogs,
he began to ignite,
> *"I will not lie down,*
> *I cannot lie down,*
> *I shall stand up and fight!*

Phase 1: Realization

"If it takes my life, so be it,
then let me die,
But on my word, before I go,
you will hear my battle cry."

And then once again,
this is going to mess up your head,
Que, stepped in,
and this is what he said,

"We won't shed blood,
with our claws or our fangs,
Instead we will evolve and revolt,
by using our brains."

When we tell this story of Que,
We began to understand,
To be excluded because of a bark,
is like being considered 3/5 of a man.

Maybe I lost you just then,
so allow me to say this once again,
Transformation doesn't start on the outside.
Lasting change starts from within.

PHASE TWO
"Rewards without risk"
The concept that doesn't exist!

"Once we rid ourselves of traditional thinking we can get on with creating the future."

---James Bertrand

This phase explores the rewards that only come as we build our self-confidence, begin to accept change, and take the necessary risk to become who we were meant to be.

Why Self-confidence?

Self-confidence plays a key role in determining our happiness. It can range from high to low depending on how honest we are with ourselves in evaluating our true abilities. Once we become confident in ourselves, we must learn to stretch our goals. This gives us the opportunity to grow beyond our comfort zones. Our comfort zones are the mental prisons that keep our minds locked away from the freedom to change.

Why Accept Change?

Change brings about growth, a whole new frontier of opportunity that is often unappreciated. This is the effect of overvaluing what we have in the present. The very things that we are afraid to give up are consistently controlling us. Until we truly understand that change is growth and that growth requires cost or something of value, we will continue to stagnate, unable to change. At some point we have to become like Que realizing "There is no evolution without a revolution." We have to take a stand against our traditional ways of thinking.

The whole concept of embracing change illustrates the power in taking risk. It is impossible for us to create a future if we continue to repeat the same cycles, never questioning the norm. Eventually, the hungry man has to decide to focus 100 percent of his energy towards capturing one chicken and face the possibility that he may fail in his endeavor. He has to come to the realization that this presents better odds than having his energy split chasing after two chickens for fear of not having a back up plan.

Why Take Risk?

The second phase of growth for me was overcoming the fear of failure. I am now aware that for the longest time I was incapable of winning because I was afraid to fail. My theory is that in life we continue to expect higher levels of comfort but are afraid to do the necessary things to realize our dreams. We come into the world defenseless, born for success; but as we grow, we become programmed to fail by societal norms. As we mature, we learn how to defend ourselves, shielding away possibilities for failure, while stunting continuous growth and opportunity for success in the process.

When we were children, our minds remained open, awaiting any information. If you can recall, our most common questions began with: Who, What, When, Where, and Why? We were eager to learn new things; we were open, welcoming growth. As we grew older, our minds began to close. We began to associate not having to ask questions with manhood/womanhood. In fact, we began to block any new information that didn't, in some way, relate to what we already thought to be the truth. We unknowingly set ourselves up to be a clone of the teachers of our youth. We became intolerant of anything that didn't agree with our (actually their) religious beliefs, ethnic and racial stereotypes, gender biases and political views. From an informational standpoint, we became the clones of our parents and immediate caregivers. This habitual reliance on what's familiar has left us one-dimensional unable to embrace the power of diversity.

A closed mind brings forth a limited perception or outlook on life. Because our perceptions are limited, the vast majority of us equate short-term failure with a permanent loss. We destroy ourselves with over-caution. We limit alternatives by refusing to take a chance and choose something different. Our lack of knowledge about risk forces us to accept that the good things coming to us from waiting are actually the leftovers of the successful people that have already made choices.

When we were young and had nothing to lose and everything to gain, we took the type of risk that it took to obtain the materials we have now. Now, that we have these basic fundamental materials, our fear of failure forces us to hold on to comfortable routines.

We continue to do the same things over and over, which brings about the same outcome.

When we get fresh information, we realize its value but we continue to use the word "but." We tell ourselves, "That sounds good in theory *but* it is not practical in the real world." "That's a good idea *but* it doesn't apply to my situation." "That's good information *but* it doesn't tell the other side of the story." As long as the situation doesn't quite fit us, we have an excuse not to change.

The only legitimate "but" is, "We know this information is true, *but* we have yet to apply it." Why should we waste time looking for the other side of the story or the negative? I think you would agree that we get enough of that daily when we turn on the television or radio. We continue to find ways to adjust the plan to our situation instead of adjusting our situation to fit the plan.

We continue to inch our way forward as if we were walking across a crowded intersection. Eventually the fear becomes so strong that we panic and stop. Frozen and unable to move, we can either stand there hoping that cars will swerve around us, or we can move forward. If we stand still, we are no longer progressing; therefore, we have no growth.

As previously mentioned, one of the most important factors of this phase is coming to the understanding of why we need to take a stand. In my situation, it was important for me to conduct a self-evaluation. In this evaluation I realized that at any given point in time I could only truly focus on one feeling or emotion.

For instance, imagine being chased by someone or something that was posing a threat to your life. If you were to trip and twist your ankle, the pain from the injury would be momentarily overshadowed by the fear of life endangerment. You would continue to run on the twisted ankle despite the pain.

When I applied this same concept to my fear of failure, I realized that I simply had to find that something that overshadowed my fear. In my case, the one thing that I fear more than failing is being thought of as "all talk and no action." So whenever I have a goal, I try to announce it to as many people as possible. No matter how great the fear of failure may be, it is nothing when compared to being associated with a dog that's all bark and no bite.

Phase 2: Rewards without Risk

Life is a series of growth cycles. Human life can be compared to that of a fruit. As long as we continue to grow, we continue to ripen. Once any fruit finds no more room for growth it eventually begins to wilt away and become rotten. In this phase, I learned that you truly have to embrace the idea that true rewards come connected with risk. Thus, I moved on to the next phase and took a note from a famous turtle named Jack.

Phase 2: Rewards without Risk

JACK

Way down deep, in the swampy bayous of Louisiana,
where the reptiles dwell,
Lived an itty, bitty turtle,
that would someday change the world.

Most have heard of the fellow,
he goes by the name of big Jack,
He was small in size, big in heart,
But on his back was a shell that was cracked.

Many have seen pictures of a man,
trapped by shackles of chains,
Not knowing the whole time, the key to his freedom,
resided in his brain.

Jack was like that fellow,
only his shackles where in the form of a shell,
He spent over half his life believing,
that this shell protected him from the world.

Growing up in the violent swamps of Louisiana,
can be a living hell,
and as a means of survival, in the sense of protection,
There should be much appreciation for his shell.

But let's be honest,
Is survival simply a means of staying a float,
in the middle of the ocean, with hopes of a potential boat?
Or does true survival consist of setting goals of reaching the shore,
with the first step of action consisting of taking strokes?

Phase 2: Rewards without Risk

Lets go from A to C, in other words,
lets skip from the details to the facts,
A shell, is a great means of protection,
but it limits growth,
which soon became a realization of Jack.

One day he grew frustrated with his cage-like shell.
Without a word of warning, to his knees he fell.

With tears in his eyes,
he looked to the skies,
asking that all important question,
"Lord, tell me, why?"

At that exact moment, he felt ashamed,
because he knew right then.
The voice of answers that he listened for outside himself,
never came,
it came, from within.

The voice spoke,

"At some point,
at some place,
at some particular time,
You've got to learn to let go!
lay it all on the line!

Rewards without risk,
is a concept that doesn't exist,
No one's going to take a chance,
on you!,
like you!,
but you!,
You know this!"

33

Phase 2: Rewards without Risk

Like the properties of water,
(conforming to the shape of its container),
or in this case, shell-like cage,
Jack focused all his energy on the weakest point,
until BAM!, he broke free in a half-crazed rage,
that left him dazed,

Depleted, and half starved,
from the knowledge that he was never fed,
He quickly revived himself,
by searching for and finding,
the key that was once lost in his head,

Maybe the story is a bit far fetched,
for the average women, or man,
For anything that lies outside the norm,
is a bit complex for them to understand.

But as we begin to connect, not physically,
but mentally
You and I become we,
as we exchange thoughts of energy

As we form covalent bonds
our thoughts become chemistry,
Set it aside, with time it marinates,
becomes one, gains synergy,

Hand in hand, we slowly dissect,
this story about Jack,
Journeying from the safe world of concrete,
to the unknown world of abstract,

Phase 2: Rewards without Risk

Not so focused, on the details,
surrounding a body of facts,
But on the growth of an individual,
daring to question why
thereby leaving his shell cracked.

Phase 2: Rewards without Risk

Phase 3: Focus

PHASE THREE

"Focus" Without Dedication, There is No Determination

"Keep away from people who belittle your ambitions. Small people always do that, but the really great make you feel that you, too, can become great."

---*Mark Twain*

This phase explores the widespread benefits of maintaining a positive attitude and how it directly relates to our focus.

The next phase for me dealt with the struggle of not reverting back to the last stage. Odds are, we all have family or friends that would like to see us remain in the cycle called "the box" along with them. Most of us have two similar but different groups of family and friends. There's no debating the fact that both love us very much, but remember, one of the groups identifies with the turtle and has grown rather fond of their shell. Their best rationalization is "other

Phase 3: Focus

people are doing it, too." In essence, they have a need to keep us in our shell to maintain the validity of their rationalization. They falsely define success based on the norm. On the other hand, the other group of family and friends isn't selfish enough to ask us to sacrifice our dreams to make them feel complete. I've divided these two groups of people into the friends that must go and the friends that must stay.

Why Not - Friends That Must Go

The friends that must go accept us as we are as long as we remain where we are. They always forgive us of our mistakes and secretly, unknowingly, hope we commit more. Their very worth as a person depends on the gratification that they get from feeling as though we need them. The strongest drive within humans is the need to feel appreciated. We all know at least one single mother that has given birth to a child in hopes that the child will make her feel complete. If not, we at least know someone that has a pet. This represents one of the few instances in life in which we actually give something without

Phase 3: Focus

expecting that it be reciprocated back to us. The truth is that they can only fulfill that urge that lies deep within each of us. We believe that the pet or the child will always love us because it needs us. Thus, we are afraid to let the child grow up or the pet roam free for fear that it may realize that it doesn't need us anymore.

The friends that must go are the best friends to have when things are going wrong. They can always relate, and the majority of the time, have a story of their own that makes us feel a little better. The problem with this negative exchange is that the whole time we swap horror stories we remain stagnant in our turtle shells. We are shielding away all the hurt, pain, and failure as well as all the joy, love, and success that comes from taking risk. Although it eases the fear to have another complacent body along side us, it is only a matter of time before the limited growth in the crowded shell begins to suffocate us.

Why - Friends That Must Stay

The friends that must stay normally possess most of the same traits as the friends that must go but for different reasons. They also accept us as we are but inspire us to evolve to our fullest potential. When things are going wrong, they are there to listen, but their approach is a little different. They give us the confidence to get back up and try again because they see the rainbow that will eventually develop from our brief stint in the rain. After reading this, we will begin to notice that when we talk about our dreams, friends that must go will become quiet, change the subject, or laugh at us as if we were silly. Friends that must stay will ask what they can do to help. We will see almost as much excitement in them as within us. The major difference is that friends that must stay tend to light up on the inside when we are happy, and friends that must go tend to light up on the inside when we are sad. I think it's obvious that we should form a preference for friends that must stay.

Power of the Mind

As I was about to exit this phase, I came to a new realization. For a moment, I was angry with the friends that must go for holding me back for so long.

Then, I realized everything happens for a reason. I began to understand the power of opposites. Every opposite exists to make you appreciate its opposite. For example, heat compliments the weakness of cold and vice versa. We can obtain a better appreciation of Chicago's winter cold, after experiencing Houston's summer heat. I began to understand that we are influenced by our surroundings whether they are positive or negative. We are ultimately responsible for which side we choose to focus on. At any given time, we have a choice as to which opposite to embrace.

Digging a Little Deeper

Up to this point, we have talked about our conscious choices of focus. These day to day decisions lie in the forefront of our thinking. Some of us are aware of these choices and have taken a proactive approach to remove the excess baggage. Fewer of us understand the ultimate power of our minds. We are so in tune with what lies in the forefront of our thinking we unknowingly discount that which lies in the background. For example, how many times have we been to the theatre and seen the

Phase 3: Focus

little cartoon drink chasing the cartoon popcorn to the concession stand. Most of us don't remember this part of the previews because it's buried in the background of our subconscious. We do, however, have an unexplainable urge to get popcorn or a drink. How many times have we been watching our favorite sitcom on television and although we are not paying much attention to the commercial breaks, we find ourselves going to the kitchen to get a refreshment? We have an urge to eat or drink that wasn't inspired by hunger. It was motivated by the subliminal messages of the commercial break.

I must admit that most mature adults (with the emphasis on mature) are capable of counteracting these subliminal messages sent to the mind; however, the mind is thrown into overdrive when it has to decipher what is real from what is fake. On the other hand, for children or people in search of themselves, the process is a bit more complicated. They don't have the necessary resources or past experiences to draw from. The mind works at optimal level when it simply brings our most prominent thoughts to reality. As I said before, the mind processes an image and creates reality as a byproduct of our most frequent thoughts. In other words we create our own reality and destiny through our thinking.

Fred W. Lowe, a motivational speaker from BMS Connections, reinforced the power of the mind to me by sharing a simple experiment during one of my class sessions. I will now share it with you. You first have to understand that for the majority of us, the mind processes information and thoughts in pictures. For instance, when we think of a win, we get a mental picture of all the things that go along with winning, using the brain's ability to associate experiences from the past. If we think of failing, we get a picture of all the things that go along with failing. Once we create the picture, our mind tries to prepare us to recreate those emotions, logic, and outcomes of whichever event. If we're unsure that we will win and our resulting thought is, "I hope I don't fail," our mind conjures up those things associated with failing. Again, the mind is capable of distinguishing the two, but it's like all at once, opening every program on your computer. It's a waste of resources, and it drains from every other

Phase 3: Focus

aspect of thinking. Besides, some of us have yet to develop the resources to handle certain scenarios.

Now, with that in mind, here is the experiment. I would like for you to pause for 30 seconds and **not** think about the difference between knowledge and education.

Phase 3: Focus

I would be willing to bet that as soon as you read that last request, you began to ponder the question, "What is the difference between knowledge and education?" The point is, even though I specifically expressed "not," and you read "not," the mind instantaneously created a mental image of your primary thoughts. It tries to bring to reality, or in this case, it ponders the question based on your past experiences. It creates mental images of the things that we have associated with knowledge and puts it against those things that we have associated with education.

I'm sure in time we could probably block it out, but this results in a waste. Time is one of the most valuable resources that we have. For all others, our kids in particular, this creates a much bigger dilemma.

For example, I was listening to the radio and heard a song with lyrics stating, "I can't pay my rent because all my money's spent, but that's all right because I'm still fly." With "fly" meaning hip and happening in this case, one is led to believe that there is something to be gained for nothing. It places focus and value on materialistic wants, such as looking good over one of the basic physiological needs, shelter. It would be easy to argue that this song is popular because it has a nice beat, and that no one really pays attention to the lyrics. In reality, subliminal messages are powerful drivers for mature adults. We cannot expect our children who are in a desperate search for role models, to have the ability to decipher this message which plays repeatedly. Imagine hearing this song ten times a day versus hearing or reading a positive message once a month. Positive has no chance to win in this setting.

Some of you may have noticed the slight drift away from the primary subject. The last paragraph illustrates how easy it is to lose focus. It also illustrates how easy it is to find your passion and make a stand. Lord Milner, one of the great colonial administrators, once said, "If we believe a thing to be bad, and if we have a right to prevent it, it is our duty to try to prevent it and damn the consequences." When you feel something, sometimes you have to just go with it. That urge to make a stand just could be your true sense of purpose trying to get you to listen. In order to maintain my focus and make my stand, I've included "Solutions" to address a current

Phase 3: Focus

problem that needs much focus. This is an optional example of how to take the first step and stand for something.

Phase 3: Focus

SOLUTIONS

Sometimes you hear a nice beat that makes you want to bob your head.
It's like getting a sniff of a home-cooked meal, but not quite being fed.

Instead, you get a little taste, you say "Yeah, I can relate,"
But it ends right there, leaving your mind in the same tranquil state.

I'm not trying to hate,
but at the very least your mind should be left a debate,
Not just recycle through negative energy
and leave you in that same place of space.

I'm up to taking the risk by saying that which most are afraid to say,
"This cycle's getting old, and it's moving at a rapid pace.

If only as a consolation, we have to drop a little information,
For art is the great teacher, the foundation for communication.

It's the gift of using words to form an illustration.
No one asks to be a role model,
but once they are, it's their obligation.

For, when it comes to communication, it starts with a contemplation,
to send a message to a listener in the form of presentation.

It takes some dedication, in addition to this stipulation,
If you feel to keep it real you need to show negative affiliations,
Also show your migration from temptation to fulfilled situations.

I wonder what would happen if I sent this to a radio station,
Would I get an excuse about
specific rules,
specific guidelines,
or regulations?

Phase 3: Focus

I can hear it now, "We don't accept solicitation,"
but they too, have an obligation.
Doesn't that come with being a part of the media?
Doesn't that define their occupation?

For me to request this to be read,
I need to come up with ten reasons why,
But when I turn on the radio, ten times a day,
they play a song titled "I Get High."

Let me ask you why?
I already know what your excuse will be,
"You just keep real, write about what's in your hood,
You write about the things that you see."

It's the same sad song,
Have you ever thought that your focus was wrong?
Instead of glorifying the negative situation,
tell us how it made you strong.

These excuses are just an illusion,
The pollution creates confusion,
Poisoning our minds when people complain and whine about problems,
but never a solution.

I've come to the conclusion,
And no,
this is not a new year's resolution.

This is a permanent substitution,
A life long constitution,
That "I do solemnly swear to use this pen for good
and make a contribution."

We can't just continue to talk about how we came up on the streets,
Let's talk about how we focus our energy into the things that we believe.

Phase 3: Focus

I could understand that we do what's necessary to get to the top,
But once we get to the top,
when does the nonsense stop?

Instead of gangsters and thugs and crying about being a victim,
Let's put our heads together and come up with a new system.

Let's talk about how when we were little
when we had these big dreams,
We never gave up on them,
which is why we achieved.

Let's take the stance when the pen is in our hands,
Never be the weakest link,
Never let down our fellow man.

It's a win-win situation and no writer will dispute it,
Because transferring thoughts,
from one party to the next is without a doubt therapeutic.

As we come to the conclusion, let me reiterate the message,
'Cause sometimes we get caught up in the rhyme scheme, but oops,
we missed it,

The intent is not to fool you,
or speak so fast that I lose you,
I'm wondering how many times,
will you press rewind,
Before something in this rhyme
begins to move you.

Well here it is simple and plain,
when you finish listening and you feel the same,
With the exception of wanting to "shake it fast,"
you have no mental stimulation or change,

Phase 3: Focus

You've just gotten high, and for the moment it dulls the pain,
But eventually it comes back to haunt you again.

This is the bottom line,
We have to stop letting them numb our minds
With these
Busted
Booty shaking,
Pointless rhymes.
Let our intellect shine.

Phase 3: Focus

Why Attitude?

I reevaluated this phase and found that this phase played a big part in teaching me about what some call "winners edge". Attitude is the one thing that separates the winners from the losers. How many times have we said, "I could have done that"? How many are reading this saying, "That's not that complicated, I could put something like that together"? The truth is twofold. Realistically, I truly believe you could have done it. It's much like setting goals; you simply have to set aside a little time to make it happen. However, the reality is that you didn't do it. I hope this inspires you to do something with whatever your talents may be. Often times the only difference between a dream and a reality is the attitude to make it happen. Rather than focussing on why you can't do something, why not focus on why you can?

Attitude describes the inner thoughts that affect our choices. We have free will to adjust our attitudes, but much too often, we are ignorant of the fact because we lack purpose. It becomes easier for us to focus on the positive when we commit ourselves to a cause, a plan, or a value system. By creating our

Phase 3: Focus

own frame of reference or paradigm, we give ourselves something to be sure of during the rough times. A well-developed attitude teaches us how to turn the bricks of life into foundations for success.

We have to learn to turn inward to adjust our attitudes so that we don't, out of laziness, continue to lean on other people and circumstances for guidance. In order for us to alter our lives, we must begin by altering our attitudes into the understanding that life has to be made into something worth living. This phase helped me to realize that I was the master of my fate. I could now soar like an eagle.

Phase 3: Focus

EAGLE

There once was a little young eagle who had trouble learning how to fly,
The truth of the matter,
or the real reason why is she use to hang out with buzzards,
the scavengers of the sky.

A buzzard's mentality, being similar to a business,
expects the most with little cost,
But when it comes to gains, in the absence of cost,
appreciation is gone, thus value's lost.

The eagle spent a lot of time with the buzzards,
in fact this comprised the majority of her day,
But a buzzard's philosophy is totally opposite an eagle;
They believe in "No Work, All Play."

With no dreams,
the buzzards were hopeless creatures often found hanging in flocks,
Every time the little eagle would attempt to fly,
they threw rocks while they laughed and mocked.

From sun up to sun down,
this went on time and time again.
It wasn't very long after this point
the little eagle began to buy in.

It was evident
she had began to believe the hype,
When she began to question herself,
saying, "Maybe the buzzards are right?"

Soon she became the laughing stock of the town,
faced with the mental choice of fight or flight.
With no support in her corner, and her confidence low,
she ran away in the middle of the night.

Phase 3: Focus

A wise old owl watched the situation unfold,
while perched on a branch from above,
But before the little eagle could get too far,
he stopped her and showed her some love.

He said,
"Don't you realize, you have been systemized,
Your hopes and dreams have all been minimized,
You've been so criticized, you have become hypnotized.
Now your doubting yourself, that's committing mental suicide.

"Rather than rush to your aid,
I waited a while to tell you this tonight,
Because the positive is best appreciated after negativity is experienced,
right?

"You know in the depths of your soul,
and in the bottom of your confused heart,
You could never appreciate the light,
until you've experienced the dark.

"I know it's hard but you have to move on,
don't think about it, just do it.
Remember,
the quickest path out of a storm headed your way
is to head directly into it.

"Now let's flip from the negative to the positive side,
You can run from the storm, but it's impossible to hide."

Before the owl could complete his thought,
the eagle turned around,
The truth,
The light,
had shined so bright,
turning her frown upside down.

Phase 3: Focus

It was no coincidence, when she returned to her residence,
No longer a little eagle, she was big with confidence.

"Hey our friend is back,"
the buzzards sang as they began their mental torture,
The eagle said,

"Hold up, fellows, I'm not the same anymore,
I've grown since my departure."

"I've grown to realize that I'm just a different breed of bird,
so full of pride, so full of culture,
The only thing
that kept me from flying before was listening to you dreamless vultures.

"I'm about to fly away, and I just want you to know
I'm not mad or filled with frustration,
After all,
it was you that pushed me to fly,
once I learned to embrace the positive as my inspiration."

The truth of the matter
is that both the negative and positive are all one in the same,
The dash represents the cost or loss, while the plus represents the gain.

They exist as two points,
illustrating the power of opposites on the life of a line,
As it moves continuous and unbroken,
in an attempt to transcend time.

As we reach for ends of the line,
and bend the line so that the two ends meet,
We create a fantastic cycle of events,
a complete circle, 360 degrees.

Phase 3: Focus

The left side of the circle exists as the negative,
which means that the positive must exist as the right,
Now it's our choice
we can choose to hop from side-to-side,
dwell in the dark or focus on the light.

Phase 3: Focus

PHASE FOUR
"Purpose" The Path to Evolution

"Strange is our situation here upon earth. Each of us comes for a short visit, not knowing why, yet sometimes seeming to divine a purpose. From the standpoint of daily life, however, there is one thing we do know: that man is here for the sake of other men."

---Albert Einstein

This phase explores the journey to find our purpose. It is a never-ending journey of trying to reach perfection, knowing all the while that it can never be obtained.

The fourth phase was definitely the longest phase. The primary focus of this phase is defining oneself. It took me about four years of pondering different thoughts before I was able to verbalize my beliefs in an efficient and effective manner. I would almost venture to say that this is one of the most important phases because it is a work-in-progress phase. It continues to transform, which means we have to continue to evolve our way of thinking to

Phase 4: Purpose

embrace its growth. Viktor Frankl, holocaust survivor and author of *Man's Search for Meaning*, wrote, "Life is never made unbearable by circumstances but only by lack of meaning and purpose."

Why Purpose?

We touched on a sense of purpose briefly in the earlier stages. In this phase, we have to come to the understanding that there is no hope in conquering anything external without first conquering that which lies within. Until we have found what we stand for, we are constantly hopping to whatever gives us a sense of external happiness and completeness. In other words, we will continually be controlled by the nice car, big house, and good job until we become one with ourselves. A sense of purpose helps us move from where we are to where we haven't been. Our bodies are built for survival and can achieve and conquer most anything, once the mind has been convinced.

Building purpose begins with building character, the foundation that people stand upon. In the tale of the three little pigs, each piglet's character was reflected in the type of house that he built. Each of the first two piglets built a house upon a weak foundation that couldn't withstand adversity. The final piglet built a house that defined who he was. Character defines who we are regardless of what we say.

It all begins by taking some initiative. We must be willing to step up and act. Taking action must become as natural as the thought of any idea. There has to come a time when we stop talking about it and start doing it. In life, the windows of opportunity are slight, forcing us to seize every opportunity. Seizing opportunities are the actions that put people in line with luck. If we seek, we shall indeed find the positive that's attached to every negative.

At some point, I think that we all reach a level of maturity where we seek to define ourselves. We grow tired of the labels placed upon us by society. When asked the question, "Who are you?" repeating our birth names, stating our title in our current profession or identifying ourselves through a relationship with someone else seems to paint an incomplete picture of who we really are. All the

Phase 4: Purpose

honors, achievements, and accolades of the past that we once used to define ourselves seem to represent such a small portion of us.

In the past, I can remember how labels given to me by external peers grew to shape me into who I thought I was. During my early years, I was a little, overly sensitive, shy kid. At that time all the neighborhood kids called me Michael Gene. Maybe they called me this because this was the terrible birth name that I was given, but I always viewed it as the name of a nerd. As I grew older and earned the title of starting linebacker for the State-Championship Chapel Hill Bulldogs, I became known as Everhart or Hart-Attack. From there, I went on to become a three year All-Conference football athlete in college. My name changed to simply HART. Towards my latter years in college, I pledged Omega Psi Phi Fraternity Inc. The letters B.I.G. were placed in front of the HART creating Big Hart, which stuck with me for a while. I'll leave it up to you to associate a mental picture with each name.

Through self-fulfilling prophecy, we try to live up to each of the titles that are placed upon us as we

Phase 4: Purpose

attempt to transform from where we are to where we would like to be. The labels represent our transitions in life. We have to take an active role in creating change for ourselves. We can't settle for becoming a product of our environment. Sometimes we have to realize that we are just a different breed of bird. As the little eagle soon realized, spending time alone is pertinent to the process of becoming all one. After a while, I reverted back to plain old Michael, a 360 degree cycle in hopes of finding my true self.

For some, we ignore this feeling of emptiness, and for others or most of you continuing to read this, this is where the process begins. The search for who we are starts with a simple vision of contemplating how we would like to be remembered. This seems to be a simple process but few people actually think ahead. In the future lies something similar but different to the very change and transition that you've run from for so long. Death is similar to change in that both represent one of the few guarantees in life. However, they differ in that death establishes an end while change establishes a beginning. Time brings about death and change, and unless we can find a

Phase 4: Purpose

way to stop time, the fight is a waste. Our best option is to embrace the inevitable and use our time wisely. Thus, we cannot wait until death is staring us in the face before we look back over life and wonder why we were here. We have to be proactive by looking forward and seeking our purpose in life.

Why Change Has To Come From Within?

Understanding the need to look forward to find purpose is the easy part. The difficult part is learning that true change has to come from within. We have to learn to be patient and take things one step at a time. I spent a large portion of my time looking for the big score, something for nothing that is. Fortunately for me, I could never find it. It's fortunate because I've come to realize that instant success without work is short term. We seldom hold something dear that cost us nothing. It is these scenarios that add validity to the statement "easy come, easy go."

There is no greater feeling than the excitement of knowing that you're putting your all into something. Not only does it clinch your efforts, but it

Phase 4: Purpose

also takes your time and embraces your faith. A sense of completeness and appreciation will fill you as you continue. Making your time and effort count for something is what you've always dreamed of. Finally, the commitment brings about a sense of security. There is no way that this endeavor will fail because it's not about the money or the fame; it's about making an honest attempt to stand for something. This chosen path is about defining who you are and adding validity to the saying, "If you can dream it, you can achieve it."

For the longest time I wondered, "What do I really love to do?" I looked inward and asked the question, "Outside of those things that I have to do, what do I spend the remainder of my time doing?" I figured that what remained would represent my true passion in life. I must admit, writing was not it. Writing this book was a nice accomplishment but merely a means to some greater ends. My true passion is philosophy, the passion for analyzing and questioning the existence of all things. As I stated before, I've always had a passion for old wise quotations, tall tales, and creative analogies. I love them so much that I unknowingly developed a talent

Phase 4: Purpose

and habit of breaking down complex material into simple analogies and short tales. I noticed that I had this desire to spend my free time in a nice brainstorming conversation exploring the different viewpoints of life.

We have to learn how to take time to get to know ourselves. We should be able to answer questions such as, "What truly makes you happy?" and "What is the one thing that you do that causes you to lose track of time?" This gives us an idea of where our passion lies.

Once we've found our passion, we have to take small steps to achieve our goal. It's very unlikely that we can go from dream to reality in one instance. Most times, we have to take some steps in between. If my ultimate dream is to host a talk show, I have to first establish some credentials. I have to realize that I don't currently have the resources to create a talk show. However, I do have the imagination to envision myself sitting and talking to each of you face to face. I can imagine that you are nodding your head in agreement or saying, "I agree with some of that, but that's not entirely true." Thus, this book becomes a step in the right direction. It will help build my

Phase 4: Purpose

credentials as a knowledgeable source on human empowerment. If my passion remains the same, this book, like money to some, becomes a mere means to a greater end.

I noticed that throughout my life, I was very careful, almost fearful, of blindly following anything or anyone. Up until I started this book, I could only remember reading two or three books completely through, start to finish. I don't say this to motivate others to do the same. In fact, I've read large portions of several books and at least five complete books since starting this endeavor. I can't expect anyone to do something that I myself am unwilling to do. I just mentioned this fact to express two points: One, I've taken extreme precaution in not allowing one school of thought to become my sole source of information because I value diversity. Two, I believe that there is little new information left to discover; power comes from the presentation of the information.

The presentation represents a combination of the best ideas. What we view as new information can be explained as a process. First, we develop a need and accumulate data. Next, we arrange the data into

Phase 4: Purpose

a format that is described as information. Finally, as we obtain more information, we are eventually considered knowledgeable on a particular subject matter. The presentation's originality depends on the messenger's ability to bring together the concepts in a manner that can move the people of his/her era. I've attempted to illustrate this point by listing various quotations of wise people from different eras.

The truth is always present, we just have to make a conscious effort to seek it or open ourselves to it. My motto became, "To seek the truth, you must question why." Thus my pen name, QUESTIONY, was born. I had now defined myself. Immediately after this realization, I reflected on something that I had heard before but didn't quite register at the time. It stated, "For where your treasure lies, there will your heart lie also." Matthew 6:21 has since helped me to find my purpose. I can't say that I have truly become one with myself because I am constantly evolving, but this newfound sense of purpose leads me in a manner much like a seeing-eye dog leads a blind man. It leads me where I want to go and shields me from harm.

Phase 4: Purpose

I don't know if you've noticed, but even my parables were transforming and evolving as I grew with each phase. We have transitioned in this conversation. As the conversation grew the pure facts began to transform into concepts. We must continue to take on more challenging tasks to stretch ourselves in all aspects of life. The best example of experiencing transitions involves a thorough examination of the life of a butterfly.

Phase 4: Purpose

BUTTERFLY

Imagine what goes on in the mind of a caterpillar,
as he waits in his cocoon to become a butterfly.
As he twists and turns, he yearns to learn
the root cause of his existence.
He questions "why?"

After careful consideration,
he comes to the realization
that meditation is the foundation
and the catalyst for metamorphosis.

Of course this
is no longer a caterpillar
yet, not quite a butterfly,
so how do we define this insect?
Could it be that he
exemplifies the Pygmalion Effect,
meaning he becomes
exactly what others expect?

Sure, he's grown a lot as a caterpillar,
seen and experienced so many things.
Maybe he's fulfilled his purpose on earth
and like an angel he has been granted some wings.

As he adapts to his immediate surroundings and environment,
he begins to grow and unfold.
Perhaps this is a fraction of the equation of life,
as he searches for purpose to become whole.

Trapped in this cocoon phase of life,
he probably feels like a locked jury,
Stuck there until he can come up with a verdict,
on what one might call the "Triple E Theory."

Phase 4: Purpose

A simple theory,
focusing on a simple realization,
We are merely products of our
environment,
        experiences, and
                expectations.

Rushing through life to become a butterfly,
important things he began to neglect.
So this cocoon was actually a blessing in disguise,
it allowed him to take time to reflect.

As a caterpillar, he was confused,
thinking that the leafy greens
measured his success.
He figured that if he could just store enough away,
he would one day find happiness.

He put everything on hold,
even his soul,
just to find these leafy greens.
He climbed tree after tree, working and saving,
thinking of the joy that they would bring.

The best excuse of all from behind which he hid,
was "I'm doing this for my family.
Build a strong foundation for my kid."

He didn't want his child to have to work so hard;
he wanted to give him all the things that he never had.
But why did his child sit home all day
doing nothing,
depending on dear old dad?

Phase 4: Purpose

He had good intentions, but the plan was incomplete,
some things were left unmapped.
The cause that he had created seemed pretty good,
but the effect was a child left handicapped.

What happened? What went wrong, we ask?
He left out one important factor.
He focused on making things easy for his child,
but surviving a struggle is what builds character.

Trying to prevent the struggle wasn't the answer,
equipping him to survive the storm was the key.
Give him the information of knowledge and education,
and a little bit of wisdom from history.

We're not focusing on the stories that we learned in school
about Columbus and all of his glory.
We're talking about history in the true sense of the word,
his-life, his-views, his-values, His-Story.

As he looked back, he knew he had made some mistakes,
there were even some he came to regret.
But the positive was knowledge of knowing,
that for every action, lies both cause and effect.

He originally thought of life as a game.
For whatever reasons all of these questions came.
His goals changed,
he was no longer the same,
and now a sense of purpose became his new aim.

He knew that he would be lost
without the answers to these few simple questions,
Acting as a map for life, serving as a sense of purpose,
pointing him in the right direction.

Phase 4: Purpose

But the answers to the questions were always there,
locked away deeply internalized,
The wings developed as knowledge acted upon
formed an education, because knowledge was applied.

Once he had fully embraced these concepts,
his wings were ready to fly.
His vision had grown from a ground level view,
to a bird's eye view from the sky.

Phase 4: Purpose

PHASE FIVE
Competing to collaborating

"The most important single ingredient in the formula of success is knowing how to get along with people."

---Theodore Roosevelt

This phase explores the many benefits of interdependency.

In phase five I discovered the unlimited power of interdependency. For me, it was necessary to experience these last two phases (developing a sense of purpose and now embracing interdependency) in the order outlined. There is no way that I could have come to rely on and trust someone else until I first learned to do so with myself. In the last phase I developed independence and moved closer to becoming whole. I learned to not allow society to define me. This was just the preparation needed to prepare me for interdependency. Unlike dependency, where you rely totally on another for support or existence, interdependency requires a mutual exchange of dependence. On a deeper level, we are all connected in some manner, which requires us to

Phase 5: Competing to Collaborating

be reciprocally dependent on one another. As demonstrated in the "Eagle" interdependency does not instruct us to revert back to leaning on the people that represent the buzzards in our life. Rather, it outlines the benefits of collaborating to achieve goals when dealing with those that characterize the owl.

I could start from so many different angles when attempting to describe this phase, but I will limit it to the two that stand out in my mind: attracting/repelling and competing/collaborating.

WHY ATTRACT?

The concept of attracting or repelling people is an old concept that was never actually associated with success or failure. It stems from the old Golden Rule, the idea that we should treat others as we would like to be treated. If we could learn to treat others the way that we would like to be treated, we would end up attracting a much greater percentage of our peers. Attracting peers makes us more persuasive by enhancing our self-confidence and increasing our visibility.

Phase 5: Competing to Collaborating

First, our peers represent our support group. No matter how confident we become in our own minds, our imperfections cause us to search for validation of our beliefs through others. Attraction is the byproduct of having a magnetic personality. When we associate with others, we give off positive energy. That force is reflected back in rewarding experiences. As we express our values and expectations through our own action, doors begin to open. Our genuine sincerity will help people trust us and want to help us. When I first began to write these short tales of life reflection, in my heart I knew that they were pretty good; but only after others began to validate my beliefs did I begin to think that they were worth sharing.

Secondly, the bigger the support groups the bigger the opportunity for success. Through others, we are able to touch people that we have never met. Regardless of how you look at it, since the dawn of time, the world has been comprised of buyers and sellers. During the days of the barter system in which knowledge was the sole source of power, the teachers acted as sellers while the students took the role of buyers. In order for a student to rise in

Phase 5: Competing to Collaborating

status, one had to show initiative in taking on the responsibilities of the teacher. In today's world, from a financial standpoint, we have to begin to take on the role of the seller. Some of us will invent and sell a product. Some of us will sell a service. Some of us will sell our ideas. Even if we choose to stay in the box, we have to sell our personalities and skills. We have to make our first impression our best.

I realized the value of impressions in the summer before the beginning of my sophomore year of college. I had just managed to maintain my proud 2.0 GPA. One of my coaches, knowing that the summer presented my only opportunity to work, called in a favor. He set me up an interview for a summer intern. I excelled in the interview and waited for the potential employer to do his routine background checks. This routine background check pulled up not one but two reasons not to hire me.

First, I had a criminal record. During the summer football practices before my freshman year, the college football team had this long distance calling code that was being passed around the athletic dorm. I, along with several other members of

Phase 5: Competing to Collaborating

the team, used the card. I was the only one foolish enough to use it from my dorm room. Because I refused to cooperate and reveal the names of my teammates, I was placed on probation for a year and charged with Class C misdemeanor.

Finally, as if that weren't enough, the interviewer called one of my former instructors. During my freshman year, I was considered a walk-on athlete. Although I had made the team and played as a true freshman, the NCAA rules stated that I couldn't formally be put on scholarship until after the first year. I had no money for books or anything else for that matter. Somehow I managed to squeak by my whole freshman year by just going to class, and taking test based on my class notes. Of course, when the interviewer asked the instructor about my work habits in an attempt to give me a second chance, the instructor labeled me a lazy, unconcerned student. Since that day I've tried to shatter the stereotype of the dumb athlete. This experience taught me that we are actions in the eyes of others.

Phase 5: Competing to Collaborating

During many of life's lessons I prematurely broke free from my cocoon. Instead of looking at situations from all angles, I quickly developed a rational for placing the blame on others. I fail to realize that all actions have a dual perspective. The person that commits an action always has a good reason for the action. To others, the reason is merely an excuse. We have to learn to take responsibility for our actions.

In a rush to become a butterfly, I missed out on many valuable lessons. Lack of patience and use of excuses caused me to redundantly repeat cycles. Fortunately in this case, I caught on fast. What once was thought to be an obstacle has manifested into a blessing. I'm fortunate that I chose to focus on the positive.

We should try to make it a point to always show people our best. Maintaining a magnetic personality becomes easier over time because there is a win-win effect in attraction. The requirements are minimal when compared to the rewards. When someone opens our eyes to new possibilities we are grateful but knowing that we have made a positive

Phase 5: Competing to Collaborating

impact on another's life is more fulfilling. I keep these ideas in the forefront of my thoughts when dealing with people in the present.

During my journeys I stumbled upon a concept called the "Six Degrees of Separation." The concept implies that every one in the world is connected via six people. To take it a step further, everyone in theory has the power to influence at least six people. Martin Luther King Junior's achievements represent our capabilities to influence others. We may not have yet mastered King's level of inspiration but we can begin by influencing six people to believe in themselves. Not only do we have to motivate six people to make a change, but also teach them to duplicate our efforts. This means that we have to encourage and coach them how to motivate and teach six others. If we are successful with a mere six, we can eventually change the world.

Why Collaboration?

The debate between competition and collaboration seems never-ending. Those arguing for competition have a main theme stating that it raises

Phase 5: Competing to Collaborating

the level of quality or performance. I can't argue against this point because I think it has validity. On a level playing field, person against person, we can raise performance and quality by creating a little rivalry between the two. The catch is we live in an imperfect world and often times the playing field is drastically tilted. We can become dominant through competition or independence, but to remain in the same dominant position requires collaboration or interdependency.

Competition requires us to remain active, not allowing us time to ponder. It is much like the box that keeps us trapped in the cycle mentioned in phase two. We have to continually feed into the cycle to maintain it. Competition requires a winner and a loser. In other words, if we don't continue to go to work for our eight hours a day, sleep for eight hours of the day to prepare us to go back to work, and split the remaining eight hours up between leisure, family and friends, we lose. In order to maintain the false sense of success, we continue to rob ourselves of time. With no time to think, we eliminate any

Phase 5: Competing to Collaborating

opportunity to develop purpose. Life without purpose is death and failure, our two greatest fears.

Collaboration embraces the pondering or merging of ideas. Collaboration puts everyone in a position to win by embracing diversity. It does not allow for one-dimensional thinking. Collaboration and competition alike are not limited to interactions with others, but they express the interactions that take place inside the individual as well.

A year ago, after I took a personality test, my results showed a strong preference towards the logical thought process of thinking over the emotional caring side of feeling. For years I had always assumed that emotions caused many people to make bad decisions. In this phase, I learned that when dealing with logic and emotion, one without the other is limited. The greatest utilization results when the energy of thinking and feeling unite to become interdependent. Emotion without logic lacks purpose resulting in an emotional flare up. Logic without emotion lacks enthusiasm which stifles its ability to move people.

Phase 5: Competing to Collaborating

No revolution in history was ever the result of a logical analysis of the situation or an emotional appeal for sympathy. As a friend once stated, "The greater good comes from that which has the greatest effect." I realized the value of interdependence within and outside of myself. The greatest effect comes from the mutual exchange of heart and mind as illustrated in the forest by the two trees.

Phase 5: Competing to Collaborating

TREES

A long time ago, in an East Texas forest,
I came across two mighty trees.
The forest had a temperature that was hot and humid
around 98.6 degrees.

One tree had branches stretching throughout the forest,
pushing life through its veins.
The other had similar branches,
but not quite the same;
its goal was to send and retrieve messages for the brain.

If the two had worked together,
they would have made a hell of a team,
But influenced heavily by society,
each tree had individual goals and dreams.

One labeled the tree of knowledge,
the other labeled the tree of life,
behaved in a manner similar to a bad marriage,
one the husband, the other the wife.

The tree of life acted mainly on emotion,
while the tree knowledge relied on the logic field.
Stubborn they were neither would yield.
When it came to any issue,
        Knowledge would say, "I think."
                Life would say, "But, I feel."

The need to feel successful and the desire to win,
were alive and present in each.
But the big picture, the view of the forest as a whole,
was clouded by the drive to compete.

Phase 5: Competing to Collaborating

There are a couple of conditions when it comes to competition,
but here is the number one rule.
It matters not the number of competitors, there's only one winner;
All others lose.

From the competitive standpoint, the concept of winning,
is all about the struggle, and the take,
Leaving an expensive fate at the end of the debate,
all competitors place their confidence at stake.

So whenever one tree would win,
it gained energy from the other tree's loss;
It would struggle to fill its cup with energy,
while the other tree paid the cost.

The concept of winning is hard for some,
and difficult for even more.
They think winning is about who crosses the finish line first
or who has the highest score.

True winning
is about giving the complete 100%,
taking the risk to go all out,
It's about laying it all on the line,
every single time,
and leaving the game with no doubts.

Don't take it wrong,
This is not to be misunderstood,
It's not all bad,
a little competition is good,

One thing should always remain in your consideration,
Too much of anything, is deemed excessive,
against the healthy balance of all things in moderation.

Phase 5: Competing to Collaborating

One day the skies became dark,
and the forest faced a terrible storm.
In order to survive, the two trees had to work together,
and defy what was then the norm.

No longer could they afford to fight it,
it was time they learn to embrace the change.
From that point on, the tree of life was now the heart,
the tree of knowledge became known as the brain.

There was a transition away from competition,
which brought about a totally new theme.
They left the feeling to the heart and the thinking to the brain,
and began to operate as a team.

At this point there was a new concept of winning,
which was all about the give and the receive.
Collaboration was their aspiration,
everyone could win,
which was something that before couldn't be achieved.

Rather than putting each other down,
they focused on lifting each other up.
The same energy that they competed for before
now began to overflow their cups.

As opposites,
the trees now reflected that which was best in each other,
Like the strength and wisdom of a father,
combined with the nourishing love of a mother.

At one point in time, their perceptions where limited,
bringing the forest to its knees.
But after filling their cups and opening their minds,
they could now view the forest through the trees.

Phase 5: Competing to Collaborating

Let us not limit this story to the struggles of man,
or even worse a forest with trees;
Let's search for more possibilities,
grow some concepts by planting some seeds.

PHASE SIX
Walking the Talk

"We are what we repeatedly do, excellence then is not an act, but a habit."

---Aristotle

This phase explores the concept of ultimate confidence (faith) and how it is maintained through discipline and persistence.

As I journeyed through the previous five phases, I remember thinking after each phase that this was it, this was the awakening that I needed. As I entered into the sixth phase the feeling of accomplishment was multiplied by ten. I finally understood that only my faith stood as a barrier between where I was and where I desired to be. Two major problems emerged as parasites eating away at my faith. First, I thought I had self-confidence but lacked self-discipline. The second is more difficult to explain, but I had been on a back and forth pendulum between the two extremes of persistence and procrastination for years. I was faced with some choices that were easier said than done.

Self-confidence under the Microscope

A conscious reader will have definitely picked up on my careful choice of words. Notice that I stated that I thought, with "thought" being the key word, that I had self-confidence. Self-confidence is definitely relative. I've always felt confident in most things that I have set out in my mind to accomplish. In other words, I've always believed with a high probability that I would be successful in my endeavors. I lacked the total confidence or without-a-doubt attitude that comes from faith.

I relate this attitude to paying tithes. Some people drop a few dollars in the church offering plate as it's passed around for tithes. Some pay tithes based on a tenth of their net income from their primary job. Others pay tithes based on a tenth of their gross income, period. Those that merely drop a few dollars in the offering think that they will be blessed for their good deed and use a considerable amount of rationalization to explain themselves. Those tithing a tenth of their net income from their primary job are pretty confident that they will be blessed for their good deed, therefore needing little rationalization. The final group pays their tithes based on a tenth of their gross earnings. There's no need for rationalization because they have faith (know without a doubt) that they will be blessed. In essence, they will their own success. Success is the result of a self-fulfilling prophecy. The final group doesn't view it as a good deed but merely a minimum requirement. I know that some people have strong feelings about their beliefs, whether for or against tithing, so don't be sidetracked by the illustration. The message is self-confidence becomes faith when you truly believe.

I realized that self-confidence is an end to the means of self-discipline. It is dependent on our ability to continue doing the small things. The little things form the infrastructure for whatever we intend to build. Ultimate confidence does not come by merely stating that you have it; it comes from having the discipline to build short successes as a foundation. It comes from having the discipline to set aside some time for yourself, to write down your goals, and create a schedule. We constantly hear people put emphasis on writing out goals and schedules but we never question why. Writing represents the embryonic stage of action. When repeated daily, it transforms into healthy habits for success.

Unfortunately, we live in the "I want it now" era. We are becoming increasingly impatient about working for something that we believe in. I don't want this to be misinterpreted, so allow me to restate this. I am not advocating working hard for someone else in hopes of rising to the top of their empire. This is a rare occurrence at best. I am advocating finding your dream and understanding that it takes time, but most importantly effort.

I thought that since I was gifted in expressing a point of view, I could breeze through writing with moderate effort. I probably could and be pretty good at it, but when you set out to accomplish any goal or dream, you have to have the discipline and desire to want to give it your all. You never get a second chance to make a first impression. Our work represents who we are and what we stand for, so we should never knowingly short change ourselves.

Again, the conscious reader probably picked up on the word "knowingly." I don't think anyone would intentionally put himself or herself at harm, but lack of knowledge and lack of persistence will often

Phase 6: Walking the Talk

hamper us. I have always been persistent in not giving up, but I haven't always been persistent in the pursuit of my dreams. Persistence and procrastination are much like the eagle dealing with the buzzards. It's only a matter of time before persistence begins to buy in to procrastination's plea to disregard time. It is true that we are our biggest competitor, but time is the thief to our success. The wisest of people wish for an opportunity to go back and do it over again. This thought alone implies that they wish they had known then what they know now. If only they would have used their time more wisely. My best friend once told me that "wisdom is wasted on the old because they lack the youth or time to formulate their thoughts into action." This implies that youth is wasted on the young, because they lack the wisdom to make it count.

The Cure for Procrastination

Procrastination eats away at our faith by telling us that the timing isn't right. That same creative justification that we used when giving tithes works in an effort to rationalize our need to wait. Eventually, we have to realize that perfection does not

Phase 6: Walking the Talk

exist. This means that the timing will never be just right. Normally, what we view as the right time is the time when we think we can win. Thus, the right time is ultimately determined by our faith in our success.

Persistence will get us over the hump. No matter how much we take in from the phases, we are impatient by nature. Because the lessons were not fully internalized or were forgotten, we will need to revisit one of these phases from time to time. Persistence reinforces the positive thinking that every lesson in some way is a blessing. From this phase, I became truly convinced that obstacles are always temporary, never permanent. Self-discipline and persistence over time are choices that build the ultimate self-confidence, faith. Thus, taking risk ultimately transforms into taking a leap of faith. No leader displays this level of self-confidence like the lion.

Phase 6: Walking the Talk

LION

There must be a lot of pressure on a lion cub
to know that one day he will be king.
No worries it seems, but they're suppressed in his dreams
regardless of the song that he sings.

Internally he's frustrated,
he keeps finding himself walking down this dark dreary trail.
Expectations are great, his reputation's at stake,
he knows he has to win, but what if he fails?

As he comes to this fork in the road,
he knows,
He can only reap that which he sows.
There's a wide path to the left
And a narrow path to the right,
of course, righteous right is the one that he chose.

He set in his heart the goal to win, saying
"I got to do the best that I can."
As times got harder and he looked over his shoulder,
there was only one set of footprints in the sand.

Just one inch too low,
      just one step too slow,
            just one more no
to a never-ending story.
Oops almost, he came so close,
but he never seemed to capture any glory.

Phase 6: Walking the Talk

He had imperfections
that needed correction,
no support from his pride
slowly loosing direction.
It was like an infection,
that was teaching him a lesson,
stealing his confidence,
and had him second-guessing.

Maybe he was too optimistic,
setting goals for himself that were not realistic.
Now he's going ballistic.

What could he say?
He kept making the same old mistakes,
his talk and walk showed no consistence.
For instance,
he could give up on this,
but he didn't want to be a hypocrite,
then he would lack in persistence.

Now he's walking around,
head hanging down,
face in the shape of a frown.
The echo of uncertainty becomes the sound
that pulls him down
as his confidence becomes lost never to be found.

He feels so alone, no one of his own,
in which he could turn to and confide.
But when he looked into the skies
he saw the stars that were always by his side.

Never wavering, always there,
even when the sun was shining so bright,
it's funny how he and we never seem to notice the stars
except in the troubles of the night.

Phase 6: Walking the Talk

There he was looking straight into the skies
afraid to ask "why" as he cried.
His thoughts were answered, but it came from inside,
this is how the stars replied:

"You split the word up wrong,
I never left you A-Lone
I only left you to become All-One,
When you saw the one set of footprints in the sand,
it was then I carried you, my son.

"Sometimes I shine,
just to remind you,
slow down don't move so quick.
Put away the sticks
and grab some bricks,
start to lay a strong foundation.
Find your cause, stand up for something
steadfast, built to last with determination.

"You're concerned about being the weakest link,
forget about what people think.
The only person you need to answer to is me.
For when you stumble and fall, it's only because
I'm preparing you for what I want you to be."

The Lion was reaching an awakening.
His body was trembling and shaking.
With the sensation bringing forth realization,
this was not merely an eye opening experience,
but the start of a transformation.

Physically he was the same,
mentally there was a little change,
but spiritually he knew the truth.
No mistaken, no more faking,
he was no longer confused.

Phase 6: Walking the Talk

He made a decision based on these conditions.
This was much bigger than a dream,
it was more like a vision.

The thing that stood out in particular,
His walk and talk were no longer perpendicular.

Walk and talk,
now had a common thought,
changing the crash course of the two rails.
Freeing him from his mental cell,
headed in the same direction,
but never intersecting
His walk and talk were now parallel.

From this came the greatest effect,
for he now demanded the respect
that he was so avidly seeking.
By changing his way of thinking,
regrouping when he felt himself sinking,
and making the effort, one day at a time,
to live in that same manner in which he was speaking.

PHASE SEVEN
"Dream and Reflect" Never Be Afraid

"Until you find something worth dying for, you are not living."

--- Unknown

This phase explores the consistent self-evaluation that must occur throughout the journey from the inside out.

Everyone encounters the six previous phases in his/ her own way. It doesn't necessarily happen in the same order, but at some point, lasting growth starts internally and works its way outward along the journey to success. This order just happens to represent the way that I've experienced it. I initially felt that the six phases were the end of my journey, but something deep within moved me to share this final phase. I guess it becomes logical on a spiritual note; seven represents the number of completion.

This final phase is hard to put into words, but it involves a self-reflection of where we stand on life's issues. Reflection builds our frame of reference, helping us find that thin line that exists between two

Phase7: Dream and Reflect

extreme positions. For example, in phase two I illustrated the benefits of confidence. There's a thin line between confidence and arrogance. In phase four I stated that true change comes from within. It requires patience and time. There's a thin line separating patience and procrastination. In phase three, I stated that we need to form a preference for the people that uplift us. There's a thin line between preference and prejudice. We saw first-hand in phase three that there's a thin line between losing focus and finding purpose. Without a conscious idea of where these lines lie, we tend to drift back and forth over the lines with no awareness of our redundant patterns.

As we slowly drift away from our destination, we wait until we have no sight of our goals before we begin to question why. We fail to realize that a lack of wisdom is the result of a lack of knowledge. A lack of knowledge is the result of a lack of information. A lack of information is the result of a lack of data. A lack of data is the result of a closed mind.

A closed mind develops when we no longer find a reason to ask why. For example, if I were to say, "It's a beautiful day outside." You would have a

Phase7: Dream and Reflect

general idea of what I mean, however you would not have a specific understanding. My definition of a beautiful day may mean that there's a cool summer breeze. Your definition may mean that it is a bright sunny day. Unless you formulate some questions, we are not quite on the same page.

If we apply this idea to a subject with more substance, such as love, we can gain a greater appreciation for the concept. We can not afford to make assumptions. It's imperative that we have a clear picture on where we stand so that we can appreciate alternative points of view without being judgmental or easily influenced. There is a thin line between being committed to an idea and being judgmental against others. A thin line also exists between being open minded and easily influenced. No one can define for us, or where we stand in the midst of the lines. We must be willing to evaluate ourselves *from the inside out.*

Whether this phase comes first, last, or sprinkled throughout the journey, it is important for us to define who we are. This is the mental preparation that gives us the confidence to make the right choices. For instance, we as humans can

Phase7: Dream and Reflect

benefit from seeing how we are like water. From one angle we know that when water finds itself in a bind, it frantically searches for the path of least resistance. This mimics most of our behaviors before we make the conscious effort to change. From another angle, we see the benefits of water's flexibility. It adapts to its environment regardless the situation. It never complains about the temperature being too cold, it simply freezes and becomes ice. Whether it's placed in a square, circular or rectangular container, it simply adapts to take the shape of its vessel. This mimics how we aspire to be. Now we just have to find a way to close the gap between the two. We merely have to make the choice to embrace the positive characteristics over the negative.

By now, the information may be starting to sound repetitive, but it takes thirty days to form a good habit and only seven days to form a bad one. How many times have we heard that our human body system requires eight glasses of water a day to run at optimum level? We continue to drink two to four. How many times have we heard of the benefits of a regular exercise regime? Shall I go on?

Phase7: Dream and Reflect

I am hoping this may act as the "accident" someone is awaiting. Maybe it will allow you to take a little time out for yourself and truly internalize the concepts in the analogies, quotes, and writings. As we have made this journey together, I have become closer to you. It allows me to open up and share a deeper side of myself. In an effort to ensure that we are on the same page, I'll leave you with a final quote and some of the pondering expressions that has occurred within my mind along the journey to free myself.

"It's their brain that I'm trying to feed, but I get this feeling that they don't much like to read. If they're not trying to hear it, I'll just hide it in some lyrics. Sometimes you have to come to the people as the people, before they will take you serious."

---Michael Everhart – QUESTIONY

Phase7: Dream and Reflect

LOVE

Two types of love, unconditional and conditional,
With the latter being a love that's highly transitional.

Unconditional love is easy to define,
but I haven't seen it in a while,
I lost my mother when I was young;
it only exists from a mother to child.

It's hard accepting the truth,
so let me make this precise,
Unconditional love can only be extended from the giver of life,
From the mother to her child,
the closest resemblance to that of Christ.

Now conditional love is relative,
which means that it needs definition.
Like I said before it can vary,
it's a love that transitions.
But this isn't
the love that we crave in the depths of our minds.
We secretly want to be loved
unconditionally
or better yet regardless of our crimes.

When we're selfish, with greed,
When we lie and when we cheat,
We want to be loved above our imperfections and dubious deeds.

If you think about it, it's kind of twisted,
we set ourselves up to fail.
Seeking unconditional love is like trying to raise bail
before going to jail.

Phase7: Dream and Reflect

The reality is
we've all been feathered, tarred, bruised, and scarred.
Although we know we should,
we have yet to drop our guards.

Some lie and cheat in false pretense,
others are afraid to put forth 100 percent.
Regardless how you look at it, our actions make no sense
because it all perpetuates the same cycle of events.

We either are unaware of the need,
or afraid to define it;
Therefore, we are doomed to assume.
We continue to give conditional love unconditional love traits,
which continues to leave us under this shadow of gloom.

It's time we break the habit.
It's time we define and compare it.
It's time we shatter the cycle,
survive with the strong.
How long will we be weak?
How long will we perish?

As we grow as friends, you become comfortable,
Slowly dropping your guard, but you feel so irresponsible
because you fear being hurt,
even worse,
you don't want to end up a fool.
You think there's a science to the madness,
Something you can learn in school,
Some sort of predefined rules.

Well listen up, friend, and I borrowed this line,
"Everybody plays the fool sometimes."

Phase7: Dream and Reflect

Avoiding the storm,
is a phrase that fills me with laughter:
No pain no gain.
When life feels like a disaster,
I'm building my character.

Romance or reality,
Romance is just a fantasy.
A fantasy is merely a vision
of how we would like things to be.
Romance consist of those sweet nothings whispered in your ear,
But the sum of all fears is what we actually see.
It brings us closer to the truth, the reality.

Conditional love is simply a level of caring,
which can be summed up as tit for tat.
It has a life cycle dependent on whether the other loves you back,
As it expands and contracts, it never seems to be exact.

'Cause when someone says "I love you,"
we associate it with our fantasy.
In our minds it's the unconditional love that we crave,
but that's not the reality.

We set up false expectations, with no realization,
That I love you means I care for you much,
"Not,"
I will be there for the duration.

I love you means I think you're a special friend,
"Not,"
I'll be there until the end.

I love you can range from hard to soft;
I love you means
I care for you until you piss me off.

Phase7: Dream and Reflect

You say,
"Love is urgent; he just hadn't experienced it yet,"
I say,
"We invalidate love by failing to define it."

Phase7: Dream and Reflect

APOLOGY

I'm sorry about those times in which you felt I disrespected you.,
I see your point of view and if in your shoes,
I'd feel neglected too.

But I'd grant you an opportunity to explain,
so I'm hoping you'd do the same
I can correct it with truth, if you'd allow me to,
clear my name of all the shame.

I'm not arguing morality,
I'm simply arguing the reality,
Sometimes our values say it's right,
but realistically that's all a fallacy.

Because actually,
the truth is simply, what it is,
it has no mind for preference.
It can hurt you, help you, and make you happy.
Truth doesn't know the difference.

And as a reference,
because of the complexity of this subject matter,
I would like to give you a sample,
An analogy of how this all plays out,
but remember this is just an example.

How is it,
that a mother could give you life and love you more than anyone else?
She'd be willing to put her life on the line and put you even before herself.

Morally she should come first in your life,
no others' wants should come before hers.
You should reciprocate that unconditional love,
at least that's what she deserves.

Phase7: Dream and Reflect

But realistically,
rivers flow downstream, never upstream and it seems,
ethics and values are powerful things,
but vanish almost as quickly as dreams.

Those images of visionary thoughts and speculation,
Have much dramatization, but little reciprocation

And the feelings of frustration
are multiplied by the thought that I let you down,
I didn't uphold my moral obligation,
so with hesitation, I scarcely come around,

I'm afraid of myself, afraid to let you down,
It's like Karma says, what goes around, comes around.

I'm at a loss for words,
I can't think of one single thing to say,
And because of your ways,
You keep extending your hand, but I keep running away

Back to my jail,
The mental cell,
My internal hell.
How can I win when I'm afraid to fail?

I guess I need to talk to someone,
and I know that if anybody, you would understand.
That's why it puzzles me to think that when the chips are down,
turning to you isn't part of the plan.

Maybe it's this urge to feel wanted and needed,
If I could fulfill that, I could feel completed.

Phase7: Dream and Reflect

But I feel defeated because you're always there;
when I win it's because you're a major component.
I just wish that I could win for once,
own it,
with no help if only for a moment.

I always knew that I needed you,
never thought that you needed me in return.
Hard lesson to learn,
but if I could take a step back into time,
the hands of time would turn.

It took me a while, but now I realize,
I could never completely push you away,
and for trying I apologize.

So during those times when those thoughts enter your mind
Which make you feel that I'm taking you for granted,
And morally we hope for a level playing field,
knowing realistically that the field is slanted,

Try to understand it,
I would never plan to hurt you, harm you, or disrespect you,
I just want someone to feel about me,
exactly the way that I feel about you.

Phase7: Dream and Reflect

RANDOM THOUGHTS

I don't want to live forever, I just want to be remembered
as someone who stood for something.
I don't want to spend 60, 70, maybe 80 years on this earth with
no meaning,
no purpose,
no nothing.

I want to stand tall in the face of controversy and challenge,
steadfast, built to last with determination,
Never a resignation,
'cause this is the ultimate measure of a man,
Affirmation of my unyielding dedication.

I don't want to grow so old that my filter becomes closed,
refusing to accept change and transition.
I want to be flexible and open to all information
with the wisdom to know when to hold my position.

I wish I had the faith to go after my dreams,
take my comfort, throw it on the crap table and bet it,
They say there's nothing in this world that man can't afford,
it's all about what he's willing to give up to get it,

I'm not going to lie, I care about what people think,
I've never been considered the weakest link,
I've got dreams that cruise as big as the Titanic
with one clause that reads "I Refuse To Sink."

I once heard a conversation about reincarnation,
but I don't know if it's the truth or a lie,
So I'm taking the stance that I don't need a second chance,
it's one shot, right now, do or die.

Phase7: Dream and Reflect

I want to go where everybody knows my name,
but don't get it twisted, I'm not looking for the fortune and fame,
I just want the opportunity to drop a few words,
a few minutes of your time so that I can be heard.

I'm tired of the societal norms and laws,
I don't want to play the game no more.
You know?
I want to tear away the puppet strings of corporate America,
· kick back and let my hair grow.

I've come to realize that there is not one single thing
that happens in this world without a reason,
Thank you experience, you've been a great teacher,
as I've journeyed through the deviations of life's seasons.

I feel consumed by this duty to do what's right,
but it's something about that urge that comes in the middle of the night.
I only added this line to show my imperfections,
to lead you otherwise would be a flagrant misdirection.

I want justification, without hesitation
of the energy that this presentation brings.
I want you to feel the quiver that flows through your soul
on Sunday morning when the choir begins to sing.

I want to turn your switch on,
make you fall into this zone,
in which all your fantasies began to roam,
you began to groan and moan,
because you never felt a feeling so strong,
and it repeats on and on and on.

What do I look for in a woman,
a topic that can go on and on for days,
I need someone beautiful, intelligent and strong,
but not so set in her ways.

Phase7: Dream and Reflect

Now when I say strong don't get me wrong,
independence is good and all,
But I've got big dreams and from time to time
I need support when I'm not feeling so tall.

A lady once said that I was afraid of my emotions,
or sharing my emotions,
and all those sort of things.
The reality is,
I didn't say what she wanted,
do what she wanted,
or sing the song that she wanted me to sing.

I'm not some parrot that sits in its cage
redundantly repeating what it hears without a care.
I'm more like a pirate in search for the treasure of truth,
yelling, "Hark! Who goes there?"

I'm different now, some things have changed,
I'm not the same as I once was before.
No more knocking to be let in, my patience is growing thin,
it's time to kick down the door.

I like to think of myself as a true observer of man,
so let me fall back on something that I was taught,
One thing that I've come to understand,
is that man has a short attention span,
so I leave you now, with a few of my random thoughts.

Coming soon
"Reflections Audio Disc"

If you thought the stories and reflections were good in the written form, just wait until you hear the audio C.D.
The audio C.D. contains the original emotions, and expressions of the author.

For more information regarding seminars & personal appearances by
Michael Everhart, visit
www.QUESTIONY.COM
or send an email to
qypublishing@sbcglobal.net

QUESTION Y PUBLISHING would like to thank you

for purchasing

FROM THE INSIDE OUT: *An Awakening*

If you would like to purchase additional copies

Send check or money order for $14.95 + $3.05

shipping and handling to

QUESTION Y PUBLISHING

P.O. Box 442005

Houston, TX 77244-2005

Or visit

www.QUESTIONY.COM

Be sure to include:

name, address, and contact number on the check or

money order.

Message from the Author

We have come to the end of this conversational journey and I hope that this experience has meant as much to you as it has meant for me. I hope this conversation has sparked something within everyone reading it. The goal of this book is two-fold. For some, this book will be a refresher of the things that they know but have yet to act upon. For others, this book will be a thought-provoking awakening.

My intentions were to write, as if I was having a face-to-face conversation with you. As the conversation progressed, I felt a strong commitment to write down exactly what I was thinking at every moment. In the middle of phase three, I felt that I neglected to uphold my moral obligation. For fear of disrupting the goal of the book I took a mental note and decided to leave it for you as an optional read. At that moment, I realized that I am not a writer or a poet. I am simply a messenger. I cannot allow myself to be confined by the technical rules of a writer or a poet. I must be free to express my message in the most effective and efficient manner possible. I have found my purpose and I must be free to serve it without restraint of traditions or norms.

Once I figured out how to get out of "the box", I felt that it was my duty to help others. It starts with first defining oneself. The first step is learning to think in terms of "I can" versus "I can't." Once we take on the "I can" attitude; it becomes easier for us to embrace the next step, taking responsibility for our actions. We have to take the responsibility to do something about our current situations. Finally, we must understand that lasting change has to start from within and move outward. We must first evolve our hearts, and minds. We have to realize that only through this path can we expect true evolution.

In the process of becoming whole, I realized that life is bigger than building financial wealth. Ultimately, along the progression of finding purpose, we find a higher cause to serve. The concept of the book, *From the Inside Out*, expresses that the cause (why) has to come first. The cause has to be bigger than me; it has to be bigger than us. Life is about starting a revolution. To truly live is to make a difference. If the time is not now, when is the time to start living? I have never felt as alive as I have been feeling in the recent moments of life. Nothing can stop me because nothing can stop us.